PAUL

DEEPENING
LIFE
TOGETHER

PAUL

LIFE TOGETHER

BakerBooks

a division of Baker Publishing Group
Grand Rapids, Michigan

Published by Baker Books
a division of Baker Publishing Group
P.O. Box 6287, Grand Rapids, MI 49516-6287
www.bakerbooks.com

Printed in the United States of America

Library of Congress Cataloging-in-Publication Data
Paul.
    p.   cm. — (Deepening life together)
    Includes bibliographical references.
    ISBN 978-0-8010-6905-5 (pbk.)
    1. Paul, the Apostle, Saint—Textbooks. 2. Bible. N.T. Epistles of Paul—Textbooks.
BS2507.P38 2011
225.9′2—dc22   2011006250

11   12   13   14   15   16   17   7   6   5   4   3   2   1

CONTENTS

ACKNOWLEDGMENTS

The *Deepening Life Together: Paul* Small Group Video Bible Study has come together through the efforts of many at Baker Publishing Group, Lifetogether Publishing, and Lamplighter Media for which we express our heartfelt thanks.

Executive Producer	John Nill
Producer and Director	Sue Doc Ross
Editors	Mark L. Strauss (Scholar), Teresa Haymaker
Curriculum Development	Brett Eastman, Sue Doc Ross, Mark L. Strauss, Teresa Haymaker, Stephanie French, Karen Lee-Thorp
Video Production	Chris Balish, Rodney Bissell, Nick Calabrese, Sebastian Hoppe Fuentes, Josh Greene, Patrick Griffin, Teresa Haymaker, Oziel Jabin Ibarra, Natali Ibarra, Janae Janik, Keith Sorrell, Lance Tracy, Sophie Olson, Ian Ross
Teachers and Scholars	Mark L. Strauss, Ben Shin, Erik Thoennes, Jon Laansma, Joanne Jung, Ken Berding, Douglas Moo, Preben Vang, Gene Green
Baker Publishing Group	Jack Kuhatschek

Special thanks to: DeLisa Ivy, Bethel Seminary, Talbot School of Theology, Wheaton College

Clips from The JESUS Film are copyright © 1995–2010 The JESUS Film Project®. A ministry of Campus Crusade for Christ International®.

Interior icons by Tom Clark

READ ME FIRST

Welcome to the *Deepening Life Together* study on *Paul*. For some of you, this might be the first time you've connected in a small group community. We want you to know that God cares about you and your spiritual growth. As you prayerfully respond to the principles you learn in this study, God will move you to a deeper level of commitment and intimacy with himself, as well as with those in your small group.

We at Baker Books and Lifetogether Publishing look forward to hearing the stories of how God changes you from the inside out during this small group experience. We pray God blesses you with all he has planned for you through this journey together.

> For the LORD is good and his love endures forever;
> his faithfulness continues through all generations.
>
> Psalm 100:5

Session Outline

Most people want to live a healthy, balanced spiritual life, but few achieve this by themselves. And most small groups struggle to balance all of God's purposes in their meetings. Groups tend to overemphasize one of the five purposes, perhaps fellowship or discipleship.

Rarely is there a healthy balance that includes evangelism, ministry, and worship. That's why we've included all of these elements in this study so you can live a healthy, balanced spiritual life over time.

A typical group session will include the following:

Memory Verses

For each session we have provided a Memory Verse that emphasizes an important truth from the session. This is an optional exercise, but we believe that memorizing Scripture can be a vital part of filling our minds with God's Word. We encourage you to give this important habit a try.

CONNECTING *with God's Family (Fellowship)*

The foundation for spiritual growth is an intimate connection with God and his family. A few people who really know you and who earn your trust provide a place to experience the life Jesus invites you to live. This section of each session typically offers you two activities.

You can get to know your whole group by using the icebreaker question, and/or you can check in with one or two group members—your spiritual partner(s)—for a deeper connection and encouragement in your spiritual journey.

DVD Teaching Segment

A *Deepening Life Together: Paul* Video Teaching DVD companion to this study guide is available. For each study session, the DVD contains a lesson taught by Mark Strauss. If you are using the DVD, you will view the teaching segment after your *Connecting* discussion and before your group discussion time (the *Growing* section).

GROWING *to Be Like Christ (Discipleship)*

Here is where you come face-to-face with Scripture. In core passages you'll explore what the Bible teaches about the topic of the study. The focus won't be on accumulating information but on how we should live in light of the Word of God. We want to help you apply the Scriptures practically, creatively, and from your heart as well as your head. At the end of the day, allowing the timeless truths from God's Word to transform our lives in Christ is our greatest aim.

DEVELOPING *Your Gifts to Serve Others (Ministry)*

Jesus trained his disciples to discover and develop their gifts to serve others. And God has designed each of us uniquely to serve him in a way no other person can. This section will help you discover and use your God-given design. It will also encourage your group to discover your unique design as a community. In this study, you'll put into practice what you've learned in the Bible study by taking a step to serve others. These simple steps will take your group on a faith journey that could change your lives forever.

SHARING *Your Life Mission Every Day (Evangelism)*

Many people skip over this aspect of the Christian life because it's scary, relationally awkward, or simply too much work for their busy schedules. But Jesus wanted all of his disciples to help outsiders connect with him, to know him personally. This doesn't mean preaching on street corners. It could mean welcoming a few newcomers into your group, hosting a short-term group in your home, or walking through this study with a friend. In this study, you'll have an opportunity to go beyond Bible study to biblical living.

SURRENDERING *Your Life for God's Pleasure (Worship)*

God is most pleased by a heart that is fully his. Each group session will give you a chance to surrender your heart to God in prayer and worship. You may read a psalm together, share a page in your journal, or sing a song to close your meeting. If you have never prayed aloud in a group before, no one will pressure you. Instead, you'll experience the support of others who are praying for you.

Study Notes

This section provides background notes on the Bible passage(s) you examine in the *Growing* section. You may want to refer to these notes during your group meeting or as a reference for those doing additional study.

For Deeper Study (optional)

Some sessions provide *For Deeper Study*. If you want to dig deeper into more Bible passages about the topic at hand, we've provided additional passages and questions. Your group may choose to do study homework ahead of each meeting in order to cover more biblical material. Or you as an individual may choose to study the *For Deeper Study* on your own. If you prefer not to do study homework, the *Growing* section will provide you with plenty to discuss within the group. These options allow individuals or the whole group to go deeper in their study, while still accommodating those who can't do homework or are new to your group. You can record your discoveries in your journal. We encourage you to read some of your insights to a friend (spiritual partner) for accountability and support. Spiritual partners may check in each week over the phone, through e-mail, or at the beginning of the group meeting.

Reflections

On the *Reflections* pages we provide Scriptures to read and reflect on between group meetings. We suggest you use this section to seek God at home throughout the week. This time at home should begin and end with prayer. Don't get in a hurry; take enough time to hear God's direction.

Subgroup for Discussion and Prayer

If your group is large (more than seven people), we encourage you to separate into groups of two to four for discussion and prayer. This is to encourage greater participation and deeper discussion.

INTRODUCTION

A Hero's Tale

Biographies of the heroes of the American Revolution are consistent bestsellers. To take just one example, you can have your pick among *American Sphinx: The Character of Thomas Jefferson* (1998); *Sworn on the Altar of God: A Religious Biography of Thomas Jefferson* (2001); or R. B. Bernstein's simply titled *Thomas Jefferson* (2003). Or perhaps you'd prefer Dumas Malone's six-volume set, *Jefferson and His Time*? Six volumes!

There's something compelling about the true story of a larger-than-life person—a complex figure who changed the course of history. Jefferson was one of those history-changing men. He penned the Declaration of Independence. He helped shape the ideas on which the American Experiment is founded. He wrote, "We hold these truths to be self-evident, that all men are created equal, that they are endowed by their Creator with certain unalienable Rights, that among these are Life, Liberty and the pursuit of Happiness." He was an inventor, an archaeologist, an ambassador, and a president.

Yet it would be hard to argue that Jefferson had more influence on the course of human history than did the apostle Paul. Just as we sometimes take the idea of human rights for granted (although it was radical in Jefferson's day), so we may take for granted Paul's radical words and deeds. But Paul, more than any other single person after Jesus, assured that Christianity became a cross-cultural movement rather than an obscure Jewish sect. He fought for the idea that one

13

did not have to convert to Judaism in order to follow Christ. He wrote much of what became the New Testament. He traveled thousands of miles on foot and by sea in order to plant the message of Christ in the key urban centers of the Roman Empire.

Saul/Paul

Paul's letters reveal a brilliant, passionate, stubborn man who cared deeply for individual people. He was born Jewish in what is now Turkey and was trained by one of the great rabbis of the age to be zealously orthodox. He fiercely fought the followers of Jesus when their movement was young. The tale of his turnaround is the stuff of drama, as are his adventures by land and sea.

In this study you'll discover:

- How Jesus invited this young hothead to change his life
- How Paul responded to God's call to share with others the message that had transformed him
- How Paul the theologian unfolds a history-changing concept
- How Paul cared for people as their pastor and mentor

Paul's two names reflect the two sides of his upbringing that became crucial in his ministry. Saul, his Jewish name, embodies his youthful immersion in the Hebrew Scriptures and the Jewish way of life. Paulus, the Roman name he had as a Roman citizen, reflects his upbringing in Tarsus, a city full of non-Jews, where Paul learned to speak fluent Greek and to relate to those outside his tight Jewish subculture. He was the ideal person to bridge the gospel from Judaism to the Roman world.

In our day, when heroes are rare and quickly attacked, we need people we can look up to as models of following Christ with courage and love. Paul is one of the greatest.

SAUL THE PERSECUTOR TURNED APOSTLE

MEMORY VERSE: Even though I was once a blasphemer and a persecutor and a violent man, I was shown mercy (1 Tim. 1:13).

"Mama worked with Papa as a medium," wrote Nicky Cruz in his 1988 autobiography, *Run Baby Run*. "Our house was the headquarters for all sorts of voodoo, séances, and sorcery."* Cruz described his childhood in Puerto Rico as full of cruelty—his father once locked him in a storage room full of scratching pigeons as punishment for theft. Eventually his parents shipped him off to New York to live with his brother, but Cruz chose a life on the streets.

After a brutal beating by a gang member and an even more brutal initiation ceremony, Cruz joined the Mau Maus, one of the most feared gangs in 1950s New York. By wits and sheer ruthlessness, he worked his way up to gang leader. When an evangelist named David Wilkerson turned up in Cruz's neighborhood and told him God loved him, Cruz threatened to kill him.

---

* Nicky Cruz with Jamie Buckingham, *Run Baby Run* (Gainesville, TX: Bridge-Logos, 1988), 4.

But Wilkerson refused to quit. "You can cut me up in a million pieces and lay them in the street," he said. "Every piece would still say I love you."

Eventually his message of God's love got through, opening Cruz to feel guilt over his sin. The day after he let Wilkerson pray with him for God's forgiveness, Cruz went to the police with some of his gang members to turn in their bricks, knives, and handguns.

Cruz went back to school and later returned to his old neighborhood as an evangelist. After serving as director for David Wilkerson's Teen Challenge, an outreach to troubled teens, he founded Nicky Cruz Outreach, touching thousands of lives over the last fifty years as a world-renowned evangelist.

Few of us have conversion stories as dramatic as Nicky Cruz's—but the apostle Paul's conversion was even more stunning. We know we're watching God at work when we see someone so full of hate change not only his beliefs but the whole direction of his life. In this session we're going to see how God broke into Paul's life to transform him from the man he was to the man he became.

 ## CONNECTING   *10 min.*

Open your group with prayer, asking God to put his finger on the areas of your life that he might want to transform through the study of Saul the persecutor. Pray that your group will gain an understanding of your faith journeys through the study of Saul's conversion.

As you begin, take time to pass around a sheet of paper on which to write down your contact information, including the best time and method for contacting you. Or pass around one of your study guides opened to the *Small Group Roster*. Then, someone volunteer to make copies or type up a list with everyone's information and e-mail it to the group this week.

1. Begin this first session by introducing yourselves. Include your name, what you do for a living, and what you do for fun. You may also include whether or not you are married, how long you have been married, how many children you have, and their ages. Also share what brought you to this *Deepening Life Together:*

16

Paul small group study and what you expect to learn during the next few weeks.

2. What is one way you're different from the kind of person you were in high school?

3. Whether your group is new or ongoing, it's always important to reflect on and review your values together. In the *Appendix* is a *Small Group Agreement* with the values we've found most useful in sustaining healthy, balanced groups. We recommend that you review these values and choose one or two—values you haven't previously focused on or have room to grow in—to emphasize during this study. Choose values that will take your group to the next stage of intimacy and spiritual health.

GROWING   *45–50 min.*

Transformation rarely comes easily, especially to passionate, stubborn people like young Saul. Stephen, a disciple of Jesus, was claiming that the system of rituals and sacrifices that God ordained through the Law of Moses had come to an end with the death and resurrection of Jesus Christ. The Jewish leaders considered Stephen's message blasphemy, so they stoned him. Saul heartily agreed with them. But change was coming.

Read Acts 7:54–8:3 aloud.

4. What can we learn about Saul from this passage?

5. Saul's passion for the Law of Moses prompted his ardent persecution of the church. When have your passions moved you to take action—in either a positive or a negative way?

Read Acts 9:1–31 aloud.

6. Saul requested the permission of the high priest to travel to Damascus. What did Saul plan to do there (vv. 1–2)?

7. On his way to Damascus, Saul was confronted with the blazing glory of Jesus Christ. He was knocked to the ground, and Jesus spoke directly to him. Why do you think Jesus revealed himself to Saul in this extraordinary way?

8. What do you suppose Saul was thinking after he heard "Saul, Saul, why do you persecute me" (v. 4)?

9. Why did Saul ask, "Who are you, Lord?" (v. 5)?

Why wasn't the speaker's identity obvious to him?

10. What do you think Saul's physical blindness signified?

11. Describe a time when God completely shocked you, or when you discovered that something you were certain was true was in fact wrong.

12. The Lord appeared to his disciple Ananias in a vision and told him to go to Saul. What was Ananias's response to God?

13. What does the Lord's statement "I will show him how much he must suffer for my name" (v. 16) say about the way the Lord was transforming Saul's life?

14. Saul embraced faith in Jesus as Messiah immediately and wholly. What were Saul's first actions as a believer?

How do those actions display the radical transformation that was under way in him?

15. In what ways was Saul still the same kind of person he had been before?

16. What can we learn about God from the fact that he called one of the worst persecutors of Jesus's followers to be one of his leading spokespeople?

Saul's transformation was from spiritual blindness to spiritual sight, from trust in himself to faith in God, and from an enemy of the church to an apostle of Jesus Christ. Saul's passion for God never diminished, but his actions were transformed, motivated by his passion for the gospel.

DEVELOPING   *10 min.*

This section is about discovering how God has designed each of us uniquely to serve him in a way no other person can—and then developing those gifts to serve others.

17. One important way to discover and develop our God-given design is to partner with another Christian for spiritual connection and accountability. We call this a spiritual partnership. We strongly recommend each of you partner with someone in the group to help you in your spiritual journey during this study. This person will be your spiritual partner for the next several weeks. He or she doesn't have to be your best friend, but will simply encourage you to complete the goals you set for yourself during this study. Following through on a resolution is tough when you're on your own, but we've found it makes all the difference to have a partner cheering us on. See the *Leader's Notes* for instructions for establishing spiritual partners. Pair up now and discuss question 18.

18. Few of us have conversion stories as dramatic as Saul's. Still, how has God changed you, or how do you think he wants to change you?

19. In the *Appendix* we've provided a *Personal Health Plan*, a chart for keeping track of your spiritual progress. You and your spiritual partner can use it for accountability to the goals you set for yourselves. See the *Personal Health Plan* for instructions. If time permits, complete the *Connect* and *Grow* questions of your *Personal Health Plan* and share your answers with your spiritual partner.

SHARING

Saul is a powerful example of God's ability to reach and save even the most impossible sinners. In Saul, God displays his mercy and unpredictability, as well as his ability to turn a person's weaknesses into strengths for ministry. Saul realized the work of Christ in his life when he said to Timothy in 1 Timothy 1:13: "Even though I was once a blasphemer and a persecutor and a violent man, I was shown mercy."

20. What does God's work in Saul's life say about the sort of people with whom we should be sharing the good news of Christ?

21. Use the *Circles of Life* diagram on page 19 to help you think of people you come in contact with on a regular basis who need to be connected in Christian community. Try to write two names in each circle. Consider the following ideas for reaching out to one or two of the people you list and make a plan to follow through with them this week:

☐ This is a wonderful time to welcome a few friends into your group. Which of the people on your list could you invite? It's possible that you may need to help your friend overcome obstacles to come to a place where he or she can encounter Jesus. Does your friend need a ride to the group or help with child care?

☐ Consider inviting a friend to attend a weekend church service with you and possibly to enjoy a meal together afterward. This can be a great opportunity to talk with someone about your faith in Jesus.

☐ Is there someone who is unable to attend your group but who still needs a connection? Would you be willing to have lunch or coffee with that person, catch up on life, and share something you've learned from this study? Jesus doesn't call all of us to lead small groups, but he does call every disciple to spiritually multiply his or her life over time.

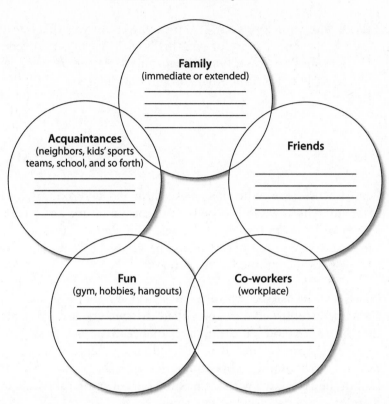

SURRENDERING

10 min.

Saul fully surrendered his heart to God. His surrender was prompted by a conversion experience that few others have experienced. As believers, we should learn all we can about what it means to surrender our lives to our Lord and then act on it.

22. Every believer should have a plan for spending time alone with God. At the end of each session, we have provided *Reflections* for you to begin daily time with him. There are five daily Scripture readings with room to record your thoughts. These will offer reinforcement of the principles we are learning and develop the habit of time alone with God throughout the week.

23. Before you close your group in prayer, answer this question: "How can we pray for you this week?" Write prayer requests on your *Prayer and Praise Report* in the *Appendix* and commit to praying for each other throughout the week.

Study Notes

Law of Moses: Embodied in Genesis through Deuteronomy, the Law of Moses tells how God chose Israel to be his people and gave them a body of legislation through Moses. The phrase "Law of Moses" can refer to these five books (also known as the Pentateuch) or to the legislation contained in these books.

Pharisee: A Jewish sect whose members came from the Jewish middle class and established and controlled the synagogues. They taught that the way to God was through obedience to the law. They opposed Jesus for a variety of reasons: he would not accept the teachings of the oral law as binding; his popularity with the people made them jealous; he associated with sinners and tax collectors; and he accused them of hypocrisy and hardheartedness.

"The Way": *The Way* is a New Testament term used to describe the beliefs and way of life of the followers of Jesus Christ.

Stoning: A form of capital punishment for certain offenses. Blasphemy is one of the offenses that required this punishment (Lev. 24:14, 16, 23).

Damascus: Damascus, a key commercial city, was located about 175 miles northeast of Jerusalem in the Roman province of Syria. Several trade routes linked Damascus to other cities throughout the Roman Empire.

Apostleship: One sent with a special message or commission. Paul is an apostle because he saw the risen Lord and was directly commissioned by him (1 Cor. 9:1; 15:8).

Ananias: A Jew who had become a believer in Christ.

Grecian: Greek-speaking. Jews who were native to the Holy Land spoke Aramaic, while those who came from other parts of the empire spoke Greek.

For Deeper Study (Optional)

What do the following passages say about the consequences of Saul's persecution of Christians?

- "But Saul began to destroy the church. Going from house to house, he dragged off men and women and put them in prison. Those who had been scattered preached the word wherever they went" (Acts 8:3–4).
- "Now those who had been scattered by the persecution in connection with Stephen traveled as far as Phoenicia, Cyprus and Antioch, telling the message only to Jews. Some of them, however, men from Cyprus and Cyrene, went to Antioch and began to speak to Greeks also, telling them the good news about the Lord Jesus. The Lord's hand was with them, and a great number of people believed and turned to the Lord" (Acts 11:19–21).
- "The church throughout Judea, Galilee and Samaria enjoyed a time of peace. It was strengthened; and encouraged by the Holy Spirit, it grew in numbers, living in the fear of the Lord" (Acts 9:31).

Reflections

Each day, give prayerful consideration to what you learn about God, his Spirit, and his place in your life. Then record your thoughts, insights, or prayer in the *Reflect* section below the verses you read. On the sixth day, record a summary of what you learned over the entire week through this study.

Day 1. You know what I was like when I followed the Jewish religion—how I violently persecuted the Christians. I did my best to get rid of them. I was one of the most religious Jews of my own age, and I tried as hard as possible to follow all the old traditions of my religion (Gal. 1:13–14 NLT).

REFLECT

_____

_____

_____

_____

Day 2. So Ananias departed and entered the house, and after laying his hands on him said, "Brother Saul, the Lord Jesus, who appeared to you on the road by which you were coming, has sent me so that you may regain your sight and be filled with the Holy Spirit" (Acts 9:17 NASB).

REFLECT

_____

_____

_____

_____

Day 3. At once he began to preach in the synagogues that Jesus is the Son of God (Acts 9:20).

REFLECT

_____

_____

_____

_____

Day 4. All those who heard him were astonished and asked, "Isn't he the man who raised havoc in Jerusalem among those who call on this name? And hasn't he come here to take them as prisoners to the chief priests?" (Acts 9:21).

REFLECT

_____

_____

_____

_____

Day 5. I thank Christ Jesus our Lord, who has strengthened me, because He considered me faithful, putting me into service, even though I was formerly a blasphemer and a persecutor and a violent aggressor. Yet I was shown mercy because I acted ignorantly in unbelief; and the grace of our Lord was more than abundant, with the faith and love which are found in Christ Jesus (1 Tim. 1:12–14 NASB).

REFLECT

_____

_____

_____

_____

Day 6. Use the following space to write any thoughts God has put in your heart and mind about the things we have looked at in this session and during your *Reflections* time this week.

SUMMARY

_____

_____

_____

_____

PAUL THE APOSTLE

MEMORY VERSE: But the Lord said to Ananias, "Go! This man is my chosen instrument to carry my name before the Gentiles and their kings and before the people of Israel" (Acts 9:15).

When Ken and Carol Lottis and Jim and Marge Petersen set out as missionaries to Brazil in 1964, they didn't go to the trackless jungles of the Amazon. Instead, they went to a bustling city in order to communicate the gospel to educated urbanites—a class of Brazilians who had largely rejected Christianity for Marxism.

Among the many challenges Ken and Jim faced was politics. A military dictatorship had taken over Brazil's government and wanted to know everything it could learn about university students who might be Marxist agitators. The American CIA was rumored to be helping the regime. And there were Ken and Jim: educated Americans with no discernable jobs and no apparent reason for their desire to hang out with Brazilian students. They didn't wear the old-fashioned clothes that people expected missionaries to wear. They didn't tote heavy Bibles. They dressed and acted like Brazilians. What else could they be but CIA?

In his book, *Will This Rock in Rio?* Ken Lottis tells how one student decided to test Jim. He had noticed that Jim was always trying to get students to read the Gospel of John with him. Always John. If Jim was out of town, Ken would pick up in the chapter of John where Jim had left off with his Bible study group. So this student wondered: If these men were CIA, then studying John was probably just their cover. Maybe that was the only part of the Bible they knew. So the student searched the Bible (an utterly foreign book to him) to find some obscure detail. Then he asked Jim, "Is there something in the Bible about a witch in a place called Endor?" Puzzled by the odd question, Jim said, "Oh yeah, that's in 1 Samuel 28." And he quickly found the passage and showed it to him. It was years later, well after his conversion, that the young man finally told Jim about his suspicions and his intended trap.

In taking the gospel to urban Brazil, Ken and Jim were following in the footsteps of Saul. Once Saul understood who Jesus was, he began to tell others, and his response to God's call led him to urban centers across the Roman Empire. Saul, the deeply Jewish persecutor, became Paul, the apostle to the Gentiles. What prompted him to step out of his comfort zone like this? And what might God's call beyond the comfort zone look like for us? That's what we'll explore in this session.

CONNECTING

10 min.

Begin your group meeting in prayer. Ask God to open your hearts and minds to an honest understanding of your motivation for following and serving Christ.

1. What is something you sometimes need to do even though it's outside your comfort zone (such as speaking in front of a large group, spending all day with toddlers, or spending time among people of another culture)?

2. Sit with your spiritual partner. If your partner is absent or if you are new to the group, join with another pair or someone who doesn't yet have a partner. (If you haven't established your

spiritual partnerships yet, turn to the *Session One Leader's Notes* in the *Appendix* for information on how to begin your partnerships.)

Turn to your *Personal Health Plan* in the *Appendix*. Share with your partner how your time with God went this week. What is one thing you discovered? Did you make a commitment to a next step that you can share? Make a note about your partner's progress and how you can pray for him or her.

GROWING

45–50 min.

In *Session One* we learned that Saul, a zealous persecutor of Christ's followers, was stopped in his tracks. On the road to Damascus, the resurrected Lord Jesus appeared to Saul and transformed him from a persecutor of Christ to a follower and an apostle. The passion and zeal Paul had exerted in persecuting Christ's church was redirected to loving and serving Christ and his church.

Read Acts 13:1–3 aloud.

3. What prompted Saul to leave Antioch and take his ministry to the outlying areas?

4. What risks and costs might Saul have faced in doing this?

5. What does "worshiping the Lord and fasting" (v. 2) have to do with receiving and responding to a call from God?

6. Have you ever sensed God's call for you to do something? If so, when?

   What were you doing when the Holy Spirit spoke?

Read Acts 13:4–12 aloud.

7. What did Saul and Barnabas do as they travelled throughout the island of Cyprus?

8. After being filled with the Holy Spirit (v. 9), Paul told the sorcerer that the Lord would blind him. This sort of thing happens often in Acts. What does this suggest about the Holy Spirit and supernatural events?

Read Acts 13:13–45 aloud.

9. Why did Paul recount the history of Israel (the exodus from Egypt, the judges, the kings—vv. 16–23) in proclaiming the good news of Jesus to this Jewish audience?

In what ways was Paul's mission successful and unsuccessful (vv. 42–45) among the people of Pisidian Antioch?

10. How bold or timid are you in speaking of Christ with non-Christians?

Why is that?

11. How do you typically react when someone rejects what you have to say?

Read Acts 13:46–52 aloud.

12. God's plan was always that all nations would come to know him through the Jewish nation (Gen. 12:3). When the Jewish leaders rejected what Paul was saying, what did he do?

Why do you think Paul responded the way he did?

13. How did the Gentiles respond to the gospel message?

How is this like, or unlike, the way people respond to the gospel message today?

14. How does Paul's example in this passage motivate you? (If it doesn't, talk about why not.)

An apostle is a messenger, an ambassador for Jesus Christ to the world. Paul took this responsibility seriously and was obedient to his calling. He never assumed responsibility for the acceptance of the message; he simply shared it obediently. He faced opposition and rejection with discouraging regularity, but remained faithful to the task and eventually saw the fruit of his labor.

SHARING

10 min.

All believers are Christ's messengers or ambassadors to the world. We are not responsible for the acceptance of the message we share, but we are to be obedient in sharing it. One thing we can learn from Paul's example is: Never give up on sharing Jesus with others, even when it seems that no one is listening.

15. God raised Jesus from the dead, and Jesus appeared to the apostles and those who had travelled with him (vv. 30–31). They became eyewitnesses that Jesus really was raised from the dead as Savior and Lord. In what sense can we be witnesses of Jesus today?

    To what group of people or area of mission has God called you? If you have no idea, how could you begin to find out?

16. Return to the *Circles of Life* and review the names of those you chose to invite to this group, to church, or for one-on-one discipleship. How did it go? Share how your invitations went. If you are attending this group for the first time because someone invited you, feel free to share your perspective on this question.
    If you haven't followed through, think about what is preventing you from doing so. As a group, consider some ways to overcome obstacles or excuses that keep us from reaching out and inviting people into our Christian community.

17. Paul's message throughout his ministry was always that through Jesus we have forgiveness of sins (vv. 38–39). Through him, everyone who believes is made right with God. Have you received God's forgiveness and justification through Christ Jesus?

    According to Paul's message, how can you be sure?

31

DEVELOPING

10 min.

Saul was motivated! He served the Lord Jesus Christ as an apostle just as passionately as he had persecuted the church before he came to know the truth of Christ as the Messiah. Saul's life became one of service to the Lord, and he encouraged others to do the same.

18. Is there an area of service that God has put on your heart to serve this group or your local church? Commit to taking the first step, and be willing to let God lead you to the ministry that expresses your passion. In your *Personal Health Plan* next to the "Develop" icon, answer the WHERE question: "WHERE are you serving?" If you are not currently serving, note one area where you will consider serving.

SURRENDERING

10 min.

19. Spend some time now surrendering your hearts to God through prayer and worship. Here are two ideas:

    ☐ Read a passage of Scripture aloud, giving God praise. You can have different people read a verse or a phrase. Consider using Psalm 147 for this exercise, or choose one of your favorite passages. The point of this exercise is to focus on God and praise him for who he is and for what he does.

    ☐ Take turns in your group completing this sentence: "Lord, I praise you for . . ."

20. Share your prayer requests in your group and then gather in smaller circles of three or four people to pray. Be sure to write down the personal requests of the members to use as a reminder to pray for your group throughout the week.

Study Notes

Antioch: Acts 10–12 tells how the church expanded when its members were scattered from Jerusalem after the initial persecution. Some of those scattered told the gospel to Gentiles as well as Jews in Antioch, a city in Syria that was one of the largest in the empire. A great number of people in the city believed, and the church in Jerusalem sent Barnabas to Antioch to assist in leadership there. Barnabas sought out Saul and brought him to Antioch, where he was a resident leader for several years. That city became the home base for his ministry.

Prophets and teachers: Simeon had the nickname Niger, which means "black." He may have come from Africa. Lucius came from what is now Libya in North Africa. Manaen was a Jew from a high social class. This was a diverse group of people.

Set apart: Dedicated.

Synagogue service: The reading of a portion of the Torah each week was the central act of congregational worship in the synagogue. This was traditionally followed by a reading from the prophets in the Jewish canon and an interpretation. A homily or sermon was then given by a visiting rabbi, a visitor from another congregation, or a well-educated member of the congregation. The tradition of inviting a visitor to give the message provided Paul with frequent invitations to preach in the synagogue.

Shake the dust off your feet: Jesus commanded this in Mark 6:11 and Matthew 10:14. The action symbolized the apostles' repudiation of those who rejected the gospel. It demonstrated that they were leaving them to God's judgment.

For Deeper Study (Optional)

1. Paul and Barnabas sailed to Perga and then on to Pisidian Antioch, where they attended the synagogue and were invited to speak. What were the key points of Paul's message to this largely Jewish audience (Acts 13:16–41)?

2. What was Paul's goal in speaking about how God led his people out of Egypt, established them in the Promised Land, and eventually gave them David as their king (Acts 13:16–23)? How are these events significant in the gospel story?

3. The idea of a crucified Messiah was hard for any Jew to swallow. What evidence did Paul give to persuade his audience that the crucified Jesus really was the Messiah (Acts 13:26–37)?

Reflections

Each day, read the daily verses and give prayerful consideration to what you learn about God, his Spirit, and his place in your life. Then record your thoughts, insights, or prayer in the *Reflect* section below the verses you read. On the sixth day record a summary of what you have learned over the entire week through this study.

Day 1. But you be watchful in all things, endure afflictions, do the work of an evangelist, fulfill your ministry (2 Tim. 4:5 NKJV).

REFLECT

_____

_____

_____

_____

Day 2. Unlike so many, we do not peddle the word of God for profit. On the contrary, in Christ we speak before God with sincerity, like men sent from God (2 Cor. 2:17).

REFLECT

_____

_____

_____

_____

Day 3. We tell you the good news: What God promised our fathers he has fulfilled for us, their children, by raising up Jesus. As it is written in the second Psalm: "You are my Son; today I have become your Father" (Acts 13:32–33).

REFLECT

_____

_____

_____

_____

Day 4. For this is what the Lord has commanded us: "I have made you a light for the Gentiles, that you may bring salvation to the ends of the earth" (Acts 13:47).

REFLECT

_____

_____

_____

_____

Day 5. And the disciples were filled with joy and with the Holy
Spirit (Acts 13:52).

REFLECT

_____

_____

_____

_____

Day 6. Use the following space to write any thoughts God has put
in your heart and mind about the things we have looked at in this
session and during your _Reflections_ time this week.

SUMMARY

_____

_____

_____

_____

PAUL THE THEOLOGIAN

MEMORY VERSE: For all have sinned and fall short of the glory of God, and are justified freely by his grace through the redemption that came by Christ Jesus (Rom. 3:23–24).

In ancient and medieval times, most people in Europe believed that harmful interactions of the planets caused disease. They thought a harmful influence or *influenza* (Italian) of the planets reached people by being carried through the air. Thus, "bad air" was blamed for disease, and people shuttered their houses when it was known to be circulating.

The idea that tiny, invisible living things might be responsible for disease took centuries to take root. In 1847, a Hungarian obstetrician named Ignaz Semmelweis was working in a hospital in Vienna and puzzling over the appallingly high rate of death (10–35 percent) from childbed fever among women who delivered at the hospital with the help of doctors. Women served by midwives were far safer. Upon investigation Semmelweis discovered that the doctors had often come to the obstetric ward straight from autopsies. He suspected that the doctors were carrying something contagious from the autopsied bodies, and he insisted that physicians wash their hands with water and lime before touching pregnant women. The incidence of childbed fever dropped to 2 percent in his hospital. Still, the Viennese medical establishment mocked his theory. It wasn't until after Semmelweis's death that Louis Pasteur definitively proved the existence of "germs."

Today we take germs for granted and wonder how educated people could ever have doubted their existence. In the same way, we may take for granted what we've been taught about what Christ's death accomplished for us. But when the apostle Paul began his ministry, the Old Testament was the only Scripture and the apostles were still thinking through the meaning of the cross. God revealed to Paul some truths that are even more important to human life than the truth of germs. In this session we'll look at some of those truths, including one whose name comes from the Roman law courts: justification.

CONNECTING
10 min.

Open your group with prayer. Ask God to help you understand what it means to be "justified" so that you can make that a reality in your lives. Thank God for how he is reshaping your group through this study.

1. Have you ever been in a situation where you needed another person to intervene to help you? It might have been an illness, an accident, a situation at school. Who did you have to rely on? What did you learn from the experience, if anything?

2. Begin to talk about what's next for your group. Do you want to continue meeting together? If so, the *Small Group Agreement* can help you talk through any changes you might want to make as you move forward. Consider what you will study, who will lead, and where and when you will meet.

GROWING
45–50 min.

Paul had a God-given ability to see how the Old Testament and Christ's death and resurrection fit together. It made him perhaps the most influential teacher of Christianity ever. Our study today will give you a taste of his theological mind at work. In Romans 3, Paul is laying out a careful explanation of how we are justified, or made right with God.

Read Romans 3:9–31 aloud. Also, scan the *Study Notes.*

3. Righteousness is the quality of being "right" before God. According to Paul in Romans 3:20, what place does the Law of Moses have in our process of becoming righteous?

How do you think the Law is able to accomplish this?

What place does the Law *not* have?

4. Paul argues that the Law and the Prophets point to a righteousness that comes from something other than law-keeping (v. 21). How does one become righteous according to verse 22?

5. When people today speak of "faith," they often mean no more than, "Yes, I believe this list of statements about Jesus." How does this compare with Paul's view of saving faith? (Consider what you learned about him in earlier sessions.)

6. Why do you think consciousness of sin (v. 20) is necessary to the process of coming to faith in Christ?

7. What has helped you become aware of sin?

8. What do you think Paul means when he says "There is no difference" (3:22) or "distinction" (NASB)?

How does this truth offer you assurance?

9. Paul says that "all have sinned and fall short of the glory of God" (v. 23). How do the non-Christians in your life respond to the assertion that their sin is a problem with eternal implications?

10. What are some attitudes or behaviors that remind us of our sinfulness?

11. Justification is the result of being made "right" before God. What does verse 24 say about how a person is justified?

12. God presented Jesus as a sacrifice of atonement, or reconciliation, to demonstrate his justice (v. 25). Read the *Study Note* on atonement. How does Jesus's sacrifice demonstrate God's justice?

13. Paul says these truths about righteousness should eliminate boasting (v. 27). Why?

14. How would your relationship to God be different without atonement and justification?

All humankind is sinful, but we can be declared righteous through Christ's death and resurrection. Christ paid the penalty that was required for our sin. Paul was the person whom God chose to think through these complex and revolutionary ideas, so that we would understand and respond to what God has done for us.

 DEVELOPING   *10 min.*

We are alive in Christ and constantly being transformed into who God wants us to be as we grow to know him more intimately.

15. Commit to taking the necessary steps to grow closer to God by beginning one of the following habits this week.

☐ *Prayer.* Commit to personal prayer and daily connection with God. You may find it helpful to write your prayers in a journal.

☐ *Reflection. Reflections* provide an opportunity for reading a short Bible passage five days a week during the course of this study. You also have the opportunity to write down your insights there. On the sixth day you can summarize what God has shown you throughout the week.

☐ *Meditation.* Try meditation as a way of internalizing God's Word more deeply. Copy a portion of Scripture on a card and tape it somewhere in your line of sight, such as your car's dashboard or the kitchen table. Think about it when you sit at red lights or while you're eating a meal. Reflect on what God is saying to you through his words. Several passages for meditation are suggested on the *Reflections* pages in each session.

16. Check in with your spiritual partner, or with another partner if yours is absent. Talk about any challenges you are currently facing in reaching the goals you set during this study. Tell your spiritual partner how he or she has helped you follow through with each step. Be sure to write down your partner's progress.

SHARING   10 *min.*

Christ wants all of his disciples to help outsiders become righteous through faith in him. Paul was a great example for us of how to accomplish this.

17. Return to the *Circles of Life* diagram and identify one or two people in each area of your life who need to know Christ. Write their names outside the circles for this exercise. Commit to praying for God's guidance and an opportunity to share with each of them.

18. Inviting people to church or Bible study is one way that we shepherd others toward faith in Christ. On your *Personal Health Plan* next to the "Share" icon, answer the "WHEN are you shepherding another person in Christ?" question.

SURRENDERING

10 min.

19. Share your prayer requests and record them on the *Prayer and Praise Report*. Have any previous prayer requests been answered? If so, celebrate these answers to prayer. Then, in simple, one-sentence prayers, submit your requests to God. Close by thanking God for his commitment to your relationship with him and how he has used this group to teach you more about righteousness.

Study Notes

Atonement: *Atonement* means a sacrifice that pays for sin. Jesus accomplished reconciliation between God and humanity by taking upon himself the penalty for our sin. Under the old covenant, animal sacrifices atoned for human sin temporarily and imperfectly. Under the new covenant, Jesus's sacrifice atones for human sin permanently and completely. Through Christ's sacrificial suffering and death, all who repent have their sins "atoned for" and forgiven.

Righteousness: *Righteousness* is the quality of being "right" with God. Christ's perfect righteousness is ascribed to believers when they accept Christ as their Savior (1 Cor. 1:30; 2 Cor. 5:20–21). Righteousness manifests as purity of heart and virtuous life, being and doing right. Because Christ bore our sin on the cross, we can be declared righteous, and we can begin a process of learning to be and do right through the power of the Holy Spirit. Romans 3 tells how we are declared righteous, while Galatians 5 addresses the process of becoming righteous in thought and action.

Justification: To be justified is to be declared righteous—or right with God. God declares us righteous not because we are innocent but because Christ paid the penalty for our sin and we put our faith in him. God declares us righteous not because our actions deserve it but because of his grace (Titus 3:4–5). Our response is faith—trust expressed through action.

Sanctification: Becoming more and more like Christ through the work of the Holy Spirit in one's life.

Grace: Undeserved acceptance and love received from another, especially God's characteristic attitude in providing salvation for sinners.*

For Deeper Study (Optional)

Read each of the following passages and explain what each one says about Christ's atonement for our sin.

- For God so loved the world that he gave his one and only Son, that whoever believes in him shall not perish but have eternal life (John 3:16).
- . . . and are justified freely by his grace through the redemption that came by Christ Jesus. God presented him as a sacrifice of atonement, through faith in his blood. He did this to demonstrate his justice, because in his forbearance he had left the sins committed beforehand unpunished (Rom. 3:24–25).
- In him we have redemption through his blood, the forgiveness of sins, in accordance with the riches of God's grace (Eph. 1:7).
- If we confess our sins, he is faithful and just and will forgive us our sins and purify us from all unrighteousness (1 John 1:9).
- This is how God showed his love among us: He sent his one and only Son into the world that we might live through him (1 John 4:9).

Read Leviticus 17:11 on the following page. Why did the atonement require shed blood?

---

* Definitions adapted from *Holman Bible Dictionary* (Nashville: Broadman & Holman), 1991.

- For the life of a creature is in the blood, and I have given it to you to make atonement for yourselves on the altar; it is the blood that makes atonement for one's life (Lev. 17:11).

Reflections

Each day, read the daily verses and give prayerful consideration to what you learn about God, his Spirit, and his place in your life. Then record your thoughts, insights, or prayer in the *Reflect* section below the verses you read. On the sixth day record a summary of what you have learned over the entire week through this study.

Day 1. Therefore, just as sin entered the world through one man, and death through sin, and in this way death came to all men, because all sinned—for before the law was given, sin was in the world. But sin is not taken into account when there is no law (Rom. 5:12–13).

REFLECT

_____

_____

_____

_____

Day 2. Create in me a pure heart, O God, and renew a steadfast spirit within me (Ps. 51:10).

REFLECT

_____

_____

_____

_____

Day 3. God made him who had no sin to be sin for us, so that in him we might become the righteousness of God (2 Cor. 5:21).

REFLECT

_____

_____

_____

_____

Day 4. Do not lie to each other, since you have taken off your old self with its practices and have put on the new self, which is being renewed in knowledge in the image of its Creator (Col. 3:9–10).

REFLECT

_____

_____

_____

_____

Day 5. And that is what some of you were. But you were washed, you were sanctified, you were justified in the name of the Lord Jesus Christ and by the Spirit of our God (1 Cor. 6:11).

REFLECT

_____

_____

_____

_____

Day 6. Use the following space to write any thoughts God has put in your heart and mind about the things we have looked at in this session and during your *Reflections* time this week.

SUMMARY

_____

_____

_____

_____

PAUL THE PASTOR-MENTOR

MEMORY VERSE: We loved you so much that we were delighted to share with you not only the gospel of God but our lives as well, because you had become so dear to us (1 Thess. 2:8).

The sturdy woman with thick glasses and a strong personality had wanted to be an overseas missionary. But instead, Henrietta Mears was in charge of Christian education at Hollywood Presbyterian Church. But "Sunday school teacher" was no dull job for Mears. Her Bible study class grew from a few dozen to six hundred college-age students each week. She also had a weekday Bible study near the UCLA campus at 6:00 a.m., and over the years she mentored hundreds of young people, including Bill and Vonette Bright, who founded Campus Crusade for Christ; Richard Halverson, who later became chaplain to the US Senate; and Billy Graham.

Full of energy even before dawn, she loudly greeted her mentorees: "Well, what's the Lord taught you since you got up this morning?" Skipping one's daily time with God was not an option.

Billy Graham said of Mears, "She has had remarkable influence, both directly and indirectly, on my life. In fact, I doubt if any other woman outside of my wife and mother has had such a marked influence."

Imagine the lasting fruitfulness of a woman who motivated and equipped Billy Graham, Bill Bright, and many others. In her role as teacher and mentor, she walked in the footsteps of the apostle Paul, who also made personal teaching and mentoring a priority. Paul invested in the lives of individuals, both new believers and young men on his ministry team. In this session we'll look at that mentoring side of Paul's work to see the qualities that can make anyone—including us—influential for Christ.

 ## CONNECTING

10 min.

Open your group with prayer. Thank God for all he has done in your group during this study. Thank him for his Word and the example Paul provides for your spiritual journey.

1. Who is one person who has helped you grow spiritually? How has he or she helped you?

2. Take time in this final session to connect with your spiritual partner. Check in with each other about the progress you have made in your spiritual growth during this study. Talk about whether you will continue in your mentoring relationship outside your Bible study group.

 ## GROWING

45–50 min.

Paul's letters demonstrate his deep concern for the church. He never stopped pastoring people and mentoring his disciples, even after he left the towns where they lived.

His letters to Thessalonica are among the earliest of his letters. They were written to the Thessalonian church, which he founded on his second missionary journey (Acts 17:1–10). The church grew quickly in both numbers and in spirituality, in spite of persecution. The Jews had stirred up virulent opposition against Paul and Silas, forcing them to flee under the cover of darkness (Acts 17:5–9). Paul was very concerned about these new believers, so he sent Timothy back to see how they were doing. Timothy did so and then reported to Paul the good news that the church in Thessalonica was thriving. Paul wrote to encourage them and to continue to guide and mentor them.

Read 1 Thessalonians 2:1–16 aloud.

3. Here Paul recalls his visit to the Thessalonians. What was the purpose of Paul and Silas's visit to Thessalonica (vv. 1–2)?

4. How does Paul describe his motives and methods as a pastor/ evangelist in verses 3–9?

5. In what ways should our motives and methods for ministry be like Paul's?

6. What impact did Paul and Silas's approach to ministry have on the Thessalonians and their faith (vv. 13–14a)?

7. Paul speaks of his gentleness toward the Thessalonians as a "mother caring for her little children" and his dealings as a "father deals with his own children" (vv. 7, 11). How did Paul act as a spiritual parent to them?

8. Which of Paul's qualities as a spiritual parent would you especially like to develop?

We've seen how Paul acted as a spiritual parent to new believers. Now let's look at how he mentored leaders. Titus was a longtime member of Paul's traveling mission team whom Paul left on the island of Crete to do a job.

Read Titus 1:5–9 aloud.

9. Why did Paul leave Titus in Crete?

10. Consider the task Paul had entrusted to Titus and the qualities he told Titus to look for in a leader. What do these suggest about Paul's opinion of Titus?

11. Paul gave Titus a list of qualifications for selecting elders in Titus 1:6–9. What does Paul's method of delegation with careful instruction teach you about spiritual mentoring?

12. Choose a quality Paul expected to see in an elder and talk about why you think it's an important one we should look for in leaders today.

13. What is one key thing you've learned about Paul from this four-session study that you'll take to heart?

For Paul, theology and ministry were about people. Think about who he was when Jesus knocked him down on the road to Damascus, and who he became. We too can make a difference in people's lives if, like Titus and the Thessalonians, we are willing to follow his example.

 ## DEVELOPING *10 min.*

Paul was effective in bringing people to relationship with the Lord and then mentoring them through their process of discovering who God created them to become as leaders. Paul was careful to teach his disciples to check their motives for serving (1 Thess. 2:5–6). We must continually ask ourselves: "Who am I really serving?" as we go about the work of Christ.

14. One way to serve Christ and his flock is through your small group. Meeting and studying God's Word together is important for the discipleship of your group members. Take some time now to consider what's next for your group as this study of Paul comes to a close. Will you continue to meet together? If so, the *Small Group Agreement* can help you talk through any changes you might want to make as you move forward. What will you study?

As your group starts a new study, this is a great time to take on a new role or change roles of service in your group. What new role will you take on? If you are uncertain, maybe your group members have some ideas for you. Remember you aren't making a lifetime commitment to the new role; it will be only for a few weeks. Also, consider sharing a role with another group member if you don't feel ready to serve solo.

SHARING   *10 min.*

To live worthy of God means to live in a way that is consistent with God's character, a way that is consistent with who we are because of faith in Christ.

15. Paul and Silas were able to help the Thessalonian believers understand what it means to live a life worthy of God. What can you do to encourage believers in your sphere of influence to live lives worthy of God?

SURRENDERING   *10 min.*

16. Close by praying for your prayer requests. Also, take a couple of minutes to review the praises you have recorded on the *Prayer and Praise Report*. Thank God for what he's done in your group during this study.

Reflections

Reading, reflecting, and meditating on the Word of God is essential to getting to know him deeply. As you read the verses each day, give prayerful consideration to what you learn about God, his Spirit, and his place in your life. Then record your thoughts, insights, or prayer in the *Reflect* section below the verses you read. On the sixth day, record a summary of what you learned over the entire week through this study.

Day 1. You are witnesses, and so is God, of how holy, righteous and blameless we were among you who believed (1 Thess. 2:10).

REFLECT

_____

_____

_____

_____

Day 2. Nobody should seek his own good, but the good of others (1 Cor. 10:24).

REFLECT

_____

_____

_____

_____

Day 3. Follow my example, as I follow the example of Christ (1 Cor. 11:1).

REFLECT

_____

_____

_____

_____

Day 4. I want to know Christ and the power of his resurrection and the fellowship of sharing in his sufferings, becoming like him in his death, and so, somehow, to attain to the resurrection from the dead (Phil. 3:10–11).

REFLECT

_____

_____

_____

_____

Day 5. What, after all, is Apollos? And what is Paul? Only servants, through whom you came to believe—as the Lord has assigned to each his task. I planted the seed, Apollos watered it, but God made it grow. So neither he who plants nor he who waters is anything, but only God, who makes things grow (1 Cor. 3:5–7).

REFLECT

_____

_____

_____

_____

Day 6. Use the following space to write any thoughts God has put in your heart and mind about the things we have looked at in this session and during your time this week.

SUMMARY

_____

_____

_____

_____

APPENDIX

FREQUENTLY ASKED QUESTIONS

What do we do on the first night of our group?
Like all fun things in life—have a party! A "get to know you" coffee, dinner, or dessert is a great way to launch a new study. You may want to review the *Small Group Agreement* and share the names of a few friends you can invite to join you. But most importantly, have fun before your study time begins.

Where do we find new members for our group?
This can be challenging, especially for new groups that have only a few people or for existing groups that lose a few people along the way. Pray with your group and then brainstorm a list of people from work, church, your neighborhood, your children's school, family, the gym, and so forth. Then have each group member invite several of the people on his or her list. Another strategy is to ask church leaders to announce that your group is open to new members.

No matter how you find members, it's vital that you stay on the lookout for new people to join your group. All groups tend to go through healthy attrition—the result of moves, releasing new leaders, ministry opportunities, and so forth—and if the group gets too small, it could be at risk of shutting down. If you and your group stay open, you'll be amazed at the people God sends your way. The next person just might become a friend for life. You never know!

How long will this group meet?
It's up to the group—once you come to the end of this study. Most groups meet weekly for at least their first six months, but every other week can work as well. We recommend that the group meet for the first six months on a weekly basis if possible. This allows for continuity, and if people miss a meeting, they aren't gone for a whole month.

At the end of this study, each group member may decide whether he or she wants to continue on for another study. Some groups launch relationships that last for years, and others are stepping-stones into another group experience. Either way, enjoy the journey.

What if this group is not working for me?

Personality conflicts, life stage differences, geographical distance, level of spiritual maturity, or any number of things can cause you to feel the group doesn't work for you. Relax. Pray for God's direction, and at the end of this study decide whether to continue with this group or find another. You don't buy the first car you look at or marry the first person you date, and the same goes with a group. Don't bail out before the study is finished—God might have something to teach you. Also, don't run from conflict or prejudge people before you have given them a chance. God is still working in you too!

Who is the leader?

Most groups have an official leader. But ideally, the group will mature and members will share the facilitation of meetings. Healthy groups share hosting and leading. This ensures that all members grow, give their unique contribution, and develop their gifts. This study guide and the Holy Spirit can keep things on track even when you share leadership. Christ has promised to be in your midst as you gather. Ultimately, God is your leader each step of the way.

How do we handle the child care needs in our group?

This can be a sensitive issue. We suggest that you empower the group to openly brainstorm solutions. Try one option that works for a while and then adjust over time. Our favorite approach is for adults to share the cost of a babysitter (or two) who can watch the kids in a different part of the house. In this way, parents don't have to be away from their young children all evening. A second option is to use one home for the kids and a second home (close by) for the adults. A third idea is to rotate the adults who provide a lesson or care for the children either in the same home or in another home nearby. This can be an incredible blessing for kids. Finally, the most common idea is to decide that you need to have a night to invest in your spiritual lives individually or as a couple, and make your own arrangements for child care. Whatever the decision, the best approach is to dialogue openly about both the problem and the solution.

SMALL GROUP CALENDAR

Planning and calendaring can help ensure the greatest participation at every meeting. At the end of each meeting, review this calendar. Be sure to include a regular rotation of host homes and leaders, and don't forget birthdays, socials, church events, holidays, and mission/ministry projects.

Date	Lesson	Dessert/Meal	Role

SMALL GROUP AGREEMENT

Our Purpose

To transform our spiritual lives by cultivating our spiritual health in a healthy small group community. In addition, we:

_____

_____

_____

Our Values

Group Attendance	To give priority to the group meeting. We will call or e-mail if we will be late or absent. (Completing the *Small Group Calendar* will minimize this issue.)
Safe Environment	To help create a safe place where people can be heard and feel loved. (Please, no quick answers, snap judgments, or simple fixes.)
Respect Differences	To be gentle and gracious to people with different spiritual maturity, personal opinions, temperaments, or imperfections. We are all works in progress.
Confidentiality	To keep anything that is shared strictly confidential and within the group, and avoid sharing improper information about those outside the group.
Encouragement for Growth	To be not just takers but givers of life. We want to spiritually multiply our lives by serving others with our God-given gifts.
Welcome for Newcomers	To keep an open chair and share Jesus's dream of finding a shepherd for every sheep.
Shared Ownership	To remember that every member is a minister and to ensure that each attender will share a small team role or responsibility over time. (See the *Team Roles*.)
Rotating Hosts/ Leaders and Homes	To encourage different people to host the group in their homes, and to rotate the responsibility of facilitating each meeting. (See the *Small Group Calendar*.)

Our Expectations

- Refreshments/mealtimes _____

- Child care _____

- When we will meet (day of week) _____

- Where we will meet (place) _____

- We will begin at (time) _____ and end at _____

- We will do our best to have some or all of us attend a worship service together. Our primary worship service time will be _____

- Date of this agreement _____

- Date we will review this agreement again _____

- Who (other than the leader) will review this agreement at the end of this study _____

TEAM ROLES

The Bible makes clear that every member, not just the small group leader, is a minister in the body of Christ. In a healthy small group, every member takes on some small role or responsibility. It can be more fun and effective if you team up on these roles.

Review the team roles and responsibilities below, and have each member volunteer for a role or participate on a team. If someone doesn't know where to serve or is holding back, as a group, suggest a team or role. It's best to have one or two people on each team so you have each of the five purposes covered. Serving in even a small capacity will not only help your leader but also will make the group more fun for everyone. Don't hold back. Join a team!

The opportunities below are broken down by the five purposes and then by a *crawl* (beginning), *walk* (intermediate), or *run* (advanced) role. Try to cover at least the crawl and walk roles, and select a role that matches your group, your gifts, and your maturity.

Team Roles	Team Player(s)

CONNECTING TEAM (Fellowship and Community Building)

Crawl: Host a social event or group activity in the first week or two.

Walk: Create a list of uncommitted friends and then invite them to an open house or group social.

Run: Plan a twenty-four-hour retreat or weekend getaway for the group.
Lead the *Connecting* time each week for the group.

GROWING TEAM (Discipleship and Spiritual Growth)

Crawl: Coordinate the spiritual partners for the group.
Facilitate a three- or four-person discussion circle during the Bible study portion of your meeting.
Coordinate the discussion circles.

Team Roles	Team Player(s)
Walk: Tabulate the *Personal Health Plans* in a summary to let people know how you're doing as a group.	
Encourage personal devotions through group discussions and pairing up with spiritual (accountability) partners.	
Run: Take the group on a prayer walk, or plan a day of solitude, fasting, or personal retreat.	

SERVING TEAM (Discovering Your God-Given Design for Ministry)

Crawl: Ensure that every member finds a group role or team he or she enjoys.	
Walk: Have every member take a gift test and determine your group's gifts.	
Plan a ministry project together.	
Run: Help each member decide on a way to use his or her unique gifts somewhere in the church.	

SHARING TEAM (Sharing and Evangelism)

Crawl: Coordinate the group's *Prayer and Praise Report* of friends and family who don't know Christ.	
Walk: Search for group mission opportunities and plan a cross-cultural group activity.	
Run: Take a small group "vacation" to host a six-week group in your neighborhood or office. Then come back together with your current group.	

SURRENDERING TEAM (Surrendering Your Heart to Worship)

Crawl: Maintain the group's *Pray and Praise Report* or journal.	
Walk: Lead a brief time of worship each week (at the beginning or end of your meeting), either a cappella or using a song from the DVD or a worship CD.	
Run: Plan a unique time of worship through Communion, foot washing, night of prayer, or nature walking.	

PERSONAL HEALTH PLAN

This worksheet could become your single most important feature in this study. On it you can record your personal priorities before the Father. It will help you live a healthy spiritual life, balancing all five of God's purposes.

You will develop your *Personal Health Plan* as you move through the study material in this study guide. At appropriate places during the study, you will be instructed to identify your progress in one or more of the purpose areas (connect, grow, develop, share, surrender) by answering the question associated with the purpose. You may be instructed to discuss with your spiritual partner your progress on one or more steps, and record your progress and the progress of your spiritual partner on the *Progress Report*.

PURPOSE	PLAN
CONNECT	WHO are you connecting with spiritually? **Bill and I will meet weekly by e-mail or phone.**
GROW	WHAT is your next step for growth? **Regular devotions or journaling my prayers 2x/week.**
DEVELOP	WHERE are you serving? **Serving in Children's Ministry** **Go through Gifts Class**
SHARE	WHEN are you shepherding another in Christ? **Shepherding Bill at lunch** **Hosting a starter group in the fall**
SURRENDER	HOW are you surrendering your heart to God? **Help with our teenager** **New job situation**

PURPOSE	PLANNING QUESTION
CONNECT	WHO are you connecting with spiritually?
GROW	WHAT is your next step for growth?
DEVELOP	WHERE are you serving?
SHARE	WHEN are you shepherding another in Christ?
SURRENDER	HOW are you surrendering your heart to God?

DATE	MY PROGRESS	PARTNER'S PROGRESS
3/5	Talked during our group	Figured out our goals together
3/12	Missed our time together	Missed our time together
3/26	Met for coffee and review of my goals	Met for coffee
4/10	E-mailed prayer requests	Praying for partner and group
5/5	Great start on personal journaling	Read Mark 1–6 in one sitting!
5/12	Traveled and not doing well this week	Journaled about Christ as healer
5/26	Back on track	Busy and distracted; asked for prayer
6/1	Need to call Children's Pastor	Scared to lead worship
6/26	Group did a serving project together	Agreed to lead group worship
6/30	Regularly rotating leadership	Led group worship–great job!
7/5	Called Jim to see if he's open to joining our group	Wanted to invite somebody, but didn't
7/12	Preparing to start a group in fall	
7/30	Group prayed for me	Told friend something I'm learning about Christ
8/5	Overwhelmed but encouraged	Absent from group today
8/15	Felt heard and more settled	Issue with wife
8/30	Read book on teens	Glad he took on his fear
9/5	Talked during our group	Figured out our goals together
9/12	Missed our time together	Missed our time together

Progress Report

DATE	MY PROGRESS	PARTNER'S PROGRESS

SERVING COMMUNION

Churches vary in their treatment of *Communion* (or *The Lord's Supper*). We offer one simple form by which a small group can share this experience together. You can adapt this as necessary, or omit it from your group altogether, depending on your church's beliefs.

Steps in Serving Communion

1. Open by sharing about God's love, forgiveness, grace, mercy, commitment, tenderheartedness, faithfulness, etc., out of your personal journey (connect with the stories of those in the room).
2. Read the passage: "And he took bread, gave thanks and broke it, and gave it to them, saying, 'This is my body given for you; do this in remembrance of me'" (Luke 22:19).
3. Pray and pass the bread around the circle.
4. When everyone has been served, remind them that this represents Jesus's broken body on their behalf. Simply state, "Jesus said, 'Do this in remembrance of me' (Luke 22:19). Let us eat together," and eat the bread as a group.
5. Then read the rest of the passage: "In the same way, after the supper he took the cup, saying, 'This cup is the new covenant in my blood, which is poured out for you'" (Luke 22:20).
6. Pray and serve the cups, either by passing a small tray, serving them individually, or having members pick up a cup from the table.
7. When everyone has been served, remind them the juice represents Christ's blood shed for them, then simply state, "Take and drink in remembrance of him. Let us drink together."
8. Finish by singing a simple song, listening to a praise song, or having a time of prayer in thanks to God.

Communion passages: Matthew 26:26–29; Mark 14:22–25; Luke 22:14–20; 1 Corinthians 10:16–21; 11:17–34

PERFORMING A FOOTWASHING

Scripture: John 13:1–17. Jesus makes it quite clear to his disciples that his position as the Father's Son includes being a servant rather than being one of power and glory only.

The Purpose of Footwashing

To properly understand the scene and the intention of Jesus, we must realize that the washing of feet was the duty of slaves and indeed of non-Jewish rather than Jewish slaves. Jesus placed himself in the position of a servant. He displayed to the disciples self-sacrifice and love. In view of his majesty, only the symbolic position of a slave was adequate to open their eyes and keep them from lofty illusions. The point of footwashing, then, is to correct the attitude that Jesus discerned in the disciples. It constitutes the permanent basis for mutual service, service in your group and for the community around you, which is laid on all Christians.

When to Implement

There are three primary places we would recommend you insert a footwashing:

- during a break in the *Surrendering* section of your group
- during a break in the *Growing* section of your group
- at the closing of your group

A special time of prayer for each person as he or she gets his or her feet washed can be added to the footwashing time.

SURRENDERING AT THE CROSS

Surrendering everything to God is one of the most challenging aspects of following Jesus. It involves a relationship built on trust and faith. Each of us is in a different place on our spiritual journey. Some of us have known the Lord for many years, some are new in our faith, and some may still be checking God out. Regardless, we all have things that we still want control over—things we don't want to give to God because we don't know what he will do with them. These things are truly more important to us than God is—they have become our god.

We need to understand that God wants us to be completely devoted to him. If we truly love God with all our heart, soul, strength, and mind (Luke 10:27), we will be willing to give him everything.

Steps in Surrendering at the Cross

1. You will need some small pieces of paper and pens or pencils for people to write down the things they want to sacrifice/surrender to God.
2. If you have a wooden cross, hammers, and nails, you can have the members nail their sacrifices to the cross. If you don't have a wooden cross, get creative. Think of another way to symbolically relinquish the sacrifices to God. You might use a fireplace to burn them in the fire as an offering to the Lord. The point is giving to the Lord whatever hinders your relationship with him.
3. Create an atmosphere conducive to quiet reflection and prayer. Whatever this quiet atmosphere looks like for your group, do the best you can to create a peaceful time to meet with God.
4. Once you are settled, prayerfully think about the points below. Let the words and thoughts draw you into a heart-to-heart connection with your Lord Jesus Christ.

   ☐ **Worship him.** Ask God to change your viewpoint so you can worship him through a surrendered spirit.

☐ **Humble yourself.** Surrender doesn't happen without humility. James 4:6–7 says, "'God opposes the proud but gives grace to the humble.' Submit yourselves, then, to God."

☐ **Surrender your mind, will, and emotions.** This is often the toughest part of surrendering. What do you sense God urging you to give him so you can have the kind of intimacy he desires with you? Our hearts yearn for this kind of connection with him; let go of the things that stand between you.

☐ **Write out your prayer.** Write out your prayer of sacrifice and surrender to the Lord. This may be an attitude, a fear, a person, a job, a possession—anything that God reveals is a hindrance to your relationship with him.

5. After writing out your sacrifice, take it to the cross and offer it to the Lord. Nail your sacrifice to the cross, or burn it as a sacrifice in the fire.
6. Close by singing, praying together, or taking communion. Make this time as short or as long as seems appropriate for your group.

Surrendering to God is life-changing and liberating. God desires that we be overcomers! First John 4:4 says, "You, dear children, are from God and have overcome . . . because the one who is in you is greater than the one who is in the world."

PRAYER AND PRAISE REPORT

Briefly share your prayer requests with the large group, making notations below. Then gather in small groups of two to four to pray for each other.

SESSION 1

Prayer Requests

_____

_____

_____

_____

Praise Reports

_____

_____

_____

_____

SESSION 2

Prayer Requests

_____

_____

_____

_____

_____

Praise Reports

_____

_____

_____

_____

_____

SESSION 3

Prayer Requests

_____

_____

_____

_____

_____

Praise Reports

_____

_____

_____

_____

_____

SESSION 4

Prayer Requests

_____

_____

_____

_____

_____

Praise Reports

_____

_____

_____

_____

LEADING FOR THE FIRST TIME
LEADERSHIP 101

Sweaty palms are a healthy sign. The Bible says God is gracious to the humble. Remember who is in control; the time to worry is when you're *not* worried. Those who are soft in heart (and sweaty palmed) are those whom God is sure to speak through.

Seek support. Ask your leader, co-leader, or close friend to pray for you and prepare with you before the session. Walking through the study will help you anticipate potentially difficult questions and discussion topics.

Bring your uniqueness to the study. Lean into who you are and how God wants you to uniquely lead the study.

Prepare. Prepare. Prepare. Go through the session several times. If you are using the DVD, listen to the teaching segment and *Leader Lifter*. Consider writing in a journal or fasting for a day to prepare yourself for what God wants to do.

Don't wait until the last minute to prepare.

Ask for feedback so you can grow. Perhaps in an e-mail or on cards handed out at the study, have everyone write down three things you did well and one thing you could improve on. Don't get defensive, but show an openness to learn and grow.

Prayerfully consider launching a new group. This doesn't need to happen overnight, but God's heart is for this to happen over time. Not all Christians are called to be leaders or teachers, but we are all called to be "shepherds" of a few someday.

Share with your group what God is doing in your heart. God is searching for those whose hearts are fully his. Share your trials and victories. We promise that people will relate.

Prayerfully consider whom you would like to pass the baton to next week. It's only fair. God is ready for the next member of your group to go on the faith journey you just traveled. Make it fun, and expect God to do the rest.

Congratulations! You have responded to the call to help shepherd Jesus's flock. There are few other tasks in the family of God that surpass the contribution you will be making. We have provided you several ways to prepare for this role. Between the *Read Me First*, these *Leader's Notes*, and the *Watch This First* and *Leader Lifter* segments on the optional *Deepening Life Together: Paul* Video Teaching DVD, you'll have all you need to do a great job of leading your group. Just don't forget, you are not alone. God knew that you would be asked to lead this group and he won't let you down. In Hebrews 13:5b God promises us, "Never will I leave you; never will I forsake you."

Your role as leader is to create a safe, warm environment for your group. As a leader, your most important job is to create an atmosphere where people are willing to talk honestly about what the topics discussed in this study have to do with them. Be available before people arrive so you can greet them at the door. People are naturally nervous at a new group, so a hug or handshake can help put them at ease. Before you start leading your group, a little preparation will give you confidence. Review the *Read Me First* at the front of your study guide so you'll understand the purpose of each section, enabling you to help your group understand it as well.

If you're new to leading a group, congratulations and thank you; this will be a life-changing experience for you also. We have provided these *Leader's Notes* to help new leaders begin well.

It's important in your first meeting to make sure group members understand that things shared personally and in prayer must remain confidential. Also, be careful not to dominate the group discussion, but facilitate it and encourage others to join in and share. And lastly, have fun.

Take a moment at the beginning of your first meeting to orient the group to one principle that undergirds this study: A healthy small group balances the purposes of the church. Most small groups emphasize Bible study, fellowship, and prayer. But God has called us to reach out to others as well. He wants us to do what Jesus teaches, not just learn about it.

Preparing for each meeting ahead of time. Take the time to review the session, the *Leader's Notes*, and the optional *Leader Lifter* for the session before each session. Also write down your answers to each question. Pay special attention to exercises that ask group members to *do* something. These exercises will help your group live out what the Bible teaches, not just talk about it. Be sure you understand how the exercises work, and bring any supplies you might need, such as paper or pens. Pray for your group members by name at least once between sessions and before each session. Use the *Prayer and Praise Report* so you will remember their prayer requests. Ask God to use your time together to touch the heart of every person. Expect God to give you the opportunity to talk with those he wants you to encourage or challenge in a special way.

Don't try to go it alone. Pray for God to help you. Ask other members of your group to help by taking on some small role. In the *Appendix* you'll find the *Team Roles* pages with some suggestions to get people involved. Leading is more rewarding if you give group members opportunities to help. Besides, helping group members discover their individual gifts for serving or even leading the group will bless all of you.

Consider asking a few people to come early to help set up, pray, and introduce newcomers to others. Even if everyone is new, they don't know that yet and may be shy when they arrive. You might give people roles like setting up name tags or handing out drinks. This could be a great way to spot a co-leader.

Subgrouping. If your group has more than seven people, break into discussion groups of three to four people for the *Growing* and *Surrendering* sections each week. People will connect more with the study and each other when they have more opportunity to participate. Smaller discussion circles encourage quieter people to talk more and tend to minimize the effects of more vocal or dominant members. Also, people who are unaccustomed to praying aloud will feel more comfortable praying within a smaller group of people. Share prayer requests in the larger group and then break into smaller groups to pray for each other. People are more willing to pray in small circles if they know that the whole group will hear all the prayer requests.

Memorizing Scripture. At the start of each session you will find a memory verse—a verse for the group to memorize each week. Encourage your group members to do this. Memorizing God's Word is both directed and celebrated throughout the Bible, either explicitly ("Your word I have hidden in my heart, that I might not sin against You" [Ps. 119:11 NKJV]), or implicitly, as in the example of our Lord ("He departed to the mountain to pray" [Mark 6:46 NKJV]).

Anyone who has memorized Scripture can confirm the amazing spiritual benefits that result from this practice. Don't miss out on the opportunity to encourage your group to grow in the knowledge of God's Word through Scripture memorization.

Reflections. We've provided opportunity for a personal time with God using the *Reflections* at the end of each session. Don't press seekers to do this, but just remind the group that every believer should have a plan for personal time with God.

Inviting new people. Cast the vision, as Jesus did, to be inclusive, not exclusive. Ask everyone to prayerfully think of people who would enjoy or benefit from a group like this—then invite them. The beginning of a new study is a great time to welcome a few people into your circle. Don't worry about ending up with too many people—you can always have one discussion circle in the living room and another in the dining room.

For Deeper Study (Optional). We have included a *For Deeper Study* section in most sessions. *For Deeper Study* provides additional passages for individual study on the topic of each session. If your group likes to do deeper Bible study, consider having members study the *For Deeper Study* passages for homework. Then, during the *Growing* portion of your meeting, you can share the high points of what you've learned.

Session One Saul the Persecutor Turned Apostle

Connecting

1. We've designed this study for both new and established groups, and for both seekers and the spiritually mature. New groups will need to invest more time building relationships with each other. Established groups often want to dig deeper into Bible study and application. Regardless of whether your group is new or has been together for a while, be sure to take time to connect at this first session.

2. Each session will include an icebreaker question that should help to set the tone for the *Growing* section of your group time. It's important in this first session to allow time for everyone to participate in this icebreaker.

3. A very important item in this first session is the *Small Group Agreement*. An agreement helps clarify your group's priorities and cast new vision for what the group can become. You can find this in the *Appendix* of this study guide. We've found that groups that talk about these values up front and commit to an agreement benefit significantly. They work through conflicts long before people get to the point of frustration, so there's a lot less pain.

   Take some time to review this agreement before your meeting. Then during your meeting, read the agreement aloud to the entire group. If some people have concerns about a specific item or the agreement as a whole, be sensitive to their concerns. Explain that tens of thousands of groups use agreements like this one as a simple tool for building trust and group health over time.

   As part of this discussion, we recommend talking about shared ownership of the group. It's important that each member have a role. See *Team Roles*. This is a great tool to get this important practice launched in your group.

   Also, you will find a *Small Group Calendar* in the *Appendix* for use in planning your group meetings and roles. Take a look at the calendar prior to your first meeting and point it out to the group so that each person can note when and where the group will meet, who will bring snacks, any important upcoming events (birthdays, anniversaries), etc.

Growing

Have someone read Bible passages aloud. It's a good idea to ask ahead of time, because not everyone is comfortable reading aloud in public.

4. Saul sided with those who killed Stephen, those who saw him as deserving death for blasphemy (Acts 8:1). He doesn't appear to have been one of those who threw the stones, but afterward he became active in the persecution of those who claimed Jesus was the Messiah (v. 3). "Going from house to house" suggests a highly active role. See the *Introduction* and *Study Notes* for more background on Saul.

6. Saul was zealous about eradicating the church. He was driven by sincere convictions about the teachings of the followers of "the Way." Not only was Saul going to pursue them, he was going to arrest both men and women and bring them back as prisoners.

7. Jesus doesn't use such tactics routinely to get people's attention. Possibly there was nothing subtler that would have gotten through to someone as hardheaded as Saul. But also, from 1 Corinthians 15:1–8 and Galatians 1:11–12 we know that Paul attached a special significance to this unique event. Seeing the resurrected Jesus in a physical manifestation qualified him to be an apostle on the level of Peter and other eyewitnesses to the resurrection, and to teach with apostolic authority. Jesus had a special mission for Saul, and for this he was called in a special way.

10. Saul's blindness possibly symbolized his spiritual blindness to the truth. His subsequent healing signifies his new insight into the truth of the gospel.

12. Ananias knew of Saul and his campaign against the church and though he recognized the Lord's voice, he was hesitant (Acts 9:13–14). Ananias went and did as the Lord commanded. Calling Saul "brother," he recounted Jesus's appearance on the road to Damascus and placed his hands on Saul so that Saul might see again and be filled with the Holy Spirit. "Immediately, something like scales fell from Saul's eyes, and he could see again" (v. 18). Saul was baptized and took some nourishment to regain his strength (vv. 18–19).

14. Very quickly, Saul started to preach in the synagogues about what he had come to believe about Jesus. This risky behavior suggests that he was fully convinced and determined to change not only his opinions but his behavior.

15. His passionate personality, religious zeal, and willingness to take bold action hadn't changed. God was simply redirecting them.

Developing

This section enables you to help the group see the importance of developing their abilities for service to God.

19. Spiritual partners will pair up during group time and/or through the week and use the *Personal Health Plan* to record plans and progress throughout our study of Paul. For many, spiritual partners will be a new idea, but we highly encourage you to try them for this study. It's hard to start a spiritual practice like prayer or consistent Bible reading with no support. A friend makes a huge difference.

   We recommend that men partner with men and women partner with women. Partners can check in with each other weekly either during your group meetings or outside the meeting. As leader, you may want to prayerfully decide who would be a good match with whom. Try to discern who might have good relational chemistry that may lead to a deeper connection. Remind people that this partnership isn't forever; it's just for a few weeks. Be sure to have extra copies of the *Personal Health Plan* available at this first meeting in case you need to have a group of three spiritual partners. It is a good idea for you to look over the *Personal Health Plan* before the meeting so you can help people understand how to use it.

Sharing

Jesus wants all of his disciples to help outsiders connect with him, to know him personally. This section should provide an opportunity to go beyond Bible study to biblical living.

21. We provided a *Circles of Life* diagram for you and the group to use to help you identify people who need to be connected in Christian community. When people are asked why they never go to church, they often say, "No one ever invited me." Remind the group that our responsibility is to invite people, but we are not responsible for how they respond. Talk to the group about the importance of inviting people; remind them that healthy small groups make a habit of inviting friends, neighbors, unconnected church members, co-workers, etc., to join their groups or join them at a weekend service. When people get connected to a group of new friends, they often join the church.

   The *Circles of Life* represent one of the values of the *Small Group Agreement*: "Welcome for Newcomers." Some groups fear that newcomers will interrupt the intimacy that members have built over time. However, groups generally gain strength with the infusion of new blood. It's like a river of living water flowing into a stagnant pond. Some groups remain permanently open, while others open periodically, such as at the beginning and ending of a study. Love grows by giving itself away. If your circle becomes too large for easy face-to-face conversations, you can simply form a second discussion circle in another room in your home.

Surrendering

God is most pleased by a heart that is fully his. Each session will provide group members a chance to surrender their hearts to God in prayer and worship. Group prayer requests and prayer time should be included every week.

22. This question is meant to encourage quiet time at home each day throughout the week. Here you can help the group see the importance of making time with God a priority. Read through this section and be prepared to help the group understand how important it is to fill our minds with the Word of God. If people already have a good Bible reading plan and commitment, that is great, but you may have people who struggle to stay in the Word daily. Sometimes beginning with a simple commitment to a short daily reading can start a habit that changes a person's life. The *Reflections* pages at the end of each session include verses that were either talked about in the session or support the teaching of the session. They are very short readings with a few lines to encourage people to write down their thoughts. Remind the group about these *Reflections* each week after the *Surrendering* section. Encourage the group to commit to a next step in prayer, Bible reading, or meditation on the Word.

23. As you move to a time of sharing prayer requests, be sure to remind the group of the importance of confidentiality and keeping what is shared in the group within the group. Everyone must feel that the personal things they share will be kept in confidence if you are to have safety and bonding among group members.

   Use the *Prayer and Praise Report* in the *Appendix* to record your prayer requests. There you can keep track of requests and celebrate answers to prayer.

For Deeper Study

We have included an optional *For Deeper Study* section in most sessions. *For Deeper Study* provides additional passages for individual study on the topic of each session. If your group likes to do deeper Bible study, consider having members study the *For Deeper Study* passages at home between meetings.

Session Two Paul the Apostle

Growing

3. The Holy Spirit spoke to the prophets and teachers in Antioch, instructing them to "set apart" Saul and Barnabas for a new calling. Saul acted in obedience to God's call.

4. Even group members not familiar with the rest of the New Testament can imagine the price Saul paid in leaving a familiar place where people knew and loved him, where he was fed and had a roof over his head, and where he was treated as a leader of a community.

7. Saul and Barnabas proclaimed the word of God in the Jewish synagogues and to government officials (Acts 13:5, 7).

8. The Holy Spirit can—and in this case did—back up the proclamation of the gospel with a demonstration of divine power. Some Christians today believe that supernatural acts of this kind were for that generation of apostles but not for today. Others believe the Holy Spirit continues to back up gospel proclamation with powerful acts like this one.

9. This history was the history of Paul's audience. He was leading up to declaring that Jesus was the descendant of David and the fulfillment of the Old Testament promises. All of this history was leading up to Jesus.

Paul's message was initially well received by all the people. But when the whole city gathered and responded favorably to Paul's message, the Jews were filled with jealousy and began to speak against it (v. 45).

12. Paul and Barnabas turned their focus to the Gentiles. Paul considered it to be a command from God. He cited Isaiah 49:6. This verse was originally addressed to all Israel, but by rejecting Jesus as Messiah, most Jews were failing to fulfill this mission to be light to the Gentiles. Paul felt that he and other Jewish followers of Christ were commanded to take up this responsibility.

13. The Gentiles were glad and honored the Word, and the Good News spread. This also happens today. New believers in the faith are often eager to share their newfound faith with others. Unfortunately, many turn away from the message as well.

Sharing

15. We too can share the good news of who Jesus is and what he has done wherever we go. If we believe the apostles' eyewitness accounts in the New Testament, and if we have a personal experience of Christ and the Holy Spirit, then we have a responsibility to tell others what we know.

Developing

18. Here is an opportunity for group members to consider where they can take a next step toward getting involved in ministering to the body of Christ in your local church. Encourage group members to use the *Personal Health Plan* to jot down their next step and plan how and when they will begin.

Session Three Paul the Theologian

Connecting

2. It's time to start thinking about what your group will do when you're finished with this study. Now is the time to ask how many people will be joining you so you can choose a study and have the books available when you meet for the next session.

Growing

3. The Law's purpose is *not* to make people declared righteous before God. Rather, the Law's purpose is to make people conscious of sin. It accomplishes this by giving people good commands that they fall short of obeying. Even a pretty good person covets things that don't belong to him, practices deceit in order to look good, and fails to love his neighbor. These acts of disobedience should show all people that they are sinners and in need of God's salvation.

4. A person receives righteousness as a gift from God when he puts "faith" in Jesus Christ.

5. The *Study Notes* define faith as "trust expressed through action." We've seen in earlier sessions that Paul expressed his faith through action. Likewise, Hebrews 11 lists a series of people who demonstrated their faith in God by doing costly things. They did not merely assent mentally to a list of beliefs. Faith involves trust in and personal allegiance to Christ, which is demonstrated in a desire for a changed life.

6. Without consciousness of our sin, we can't repent (change our minds and our direction of life) and accept Christ's forgiveness. We must recognize and acknowledge our need for forgiveness before we can ask for and accept it.

7. Some of us become aware that we have persistent habits of wrongdoing because our parents point out those habits. For many of us, reading the Scriptures or hearing them taught helps us see our sin.

8. Righteousness through faith is available *to all* who believe in Jesus regardless of our past behaviors or background.

9. Many people today can't relate to the idea that they are "sinners." They know they do wrong things from time to time, but the idea that they're bad enough to deserve eternal exclusion from God's presence may seem nonsensical or offensive. Some don't believe God exists, while others believe he exists but doesn't expect more from them than a basically decent life.

10. Try to think of some common sins: deceit (hiding the truth from others, pretending to be better than we are, letting others believe what isn't true); malice (disliking someone enough to hope that something bad happens to them); gossip; indifference to those in need; and so on. "For all have sinned and fall short" (Rom. 3:23) applies to everyone, Jews and Gentiles alike. Unless we are made right with God through Christ, sin will keep us from the presence of God. We may see degrees of sin in our lives, but all sin makes us sinners, cutting us off from God.

11. Justification is freely given by God's grace. We are redeemed by Jesus Christ, who died on the cross as a sacrifice to atone for our sin.

12. A sacrifice of atonement is a sacrifice that pays the penalty for the sins of others. God didn't just disregard our wrongdoing. He took seriously the requirement of justice: crimes demand consequences. Jesus took the eternal consequences on himself.

Sharing

17. It is important to return to the *Circles of Life* and engage the group in identifying people who need to know Christ more deeply. Encourage a commitment to praying for God's guidance and an opportunity to share with each person named in the *Circles*.

Session Four Paul the Pastor-Mentor

Growing

3. They were in Thessalonica to share the gospel of Jesus Christ. They dared to share the gospel with the Thessalonians in spite of the opposition they faced.

4. Paul says his motives were not impure (1 Thess. 2:3). He was motivated by love (v. 8), by the desire to please God (v. 4), and by the desire to fulfill God's trust in him (v. 4). They didn't use any form of manipulation or coercion, and they went out of their way to show that they weren't motivated by the desire for money or praise (v. 6).

5. We too should care about pleasing God and doing something with what God has entrusted to us. We too should be motivated by love for those who need to hear the gospel. We should care about avoiding impure motives or

manipulating others. We should have Paul's delight in sharing our lives with others.

6. If Paul and Silas had shared the gospel with them yet lived carelessly among them, the Thessalonians would have been dissuaded by hypocrisy. But because they were aware of the team's pure, honest, and faultless conduct, they embraced the gospel and mimicked the behavior they witnessed. They had seen what a true believer looks like, and they followed that example.

7. Paul acted with gentleness and love, just as God the Father deals with his children in grace. He was concerned with the Thessalonians' character development and eternal salvation. He encouraged and counseled them with the Father's affection rather than with an authoritarian hand.

9. He left him to appoint elders to lead the young church there and to "straighten out what was left unfinished" (Titus 1:5) in establishing a stable and lasting community of believers. These elders couldn't be just anyone who happened to be of high social status; they had to have strong character qualities and accurate faith.

10. Apparently he trusted that Titus was capable of completing the work of appointing elders in each town. He had the discernment to choose men of high character with a firm understanding of the gospel and the ability to handle opposition. It's reasonable to infer that Titus had those qualities as well.

Sharing

15. One of the best things you can do is to set an example—if you do what Paul did, then others will do what you are doing.

SMALL GROUP ROSTER

Name	Address	Phone	E-mail Address	Team or Role	When/How to Contact You

Pass your book around your group at your first meeting to get every-one's name and contact information.

Name	Address	Phone	E-mail Address	Team or Role	When/How to Contact You

DEEPENING LIFE TOGETHER SERIES

Six **NEW** Studies Now Available!

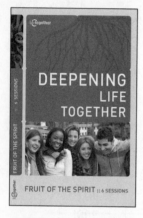

FRUIT OF THE SPIRIT

JAMES

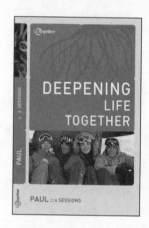

PAUL

PSALMS

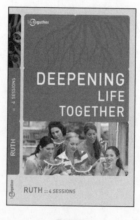

RUTH

SERMON ON THE MOUNT

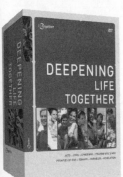